SUPERBIKES

IAN GRAHAM

Heinemann Library
Chicago, Illinois

Design by Jo Hinton-Malivoire and Tinstar Design Limited (www.tinstar.co.uk)
Illustrations by Geoff Ward
Originated by Dot Gradations Ltd
Printed and bound in Hong Kong, China, by South China Printing

07 06 05 04 03
10 9 8 7 6 5 4 3 2 1

Library of Congress Cataloging-in-Publication Data
Graham, Ian, 1953-
    Superbikes / Ian Graham. -- Chicago, IL; Heinemann Library, 2003.
32 p. : col. ill. ; p. cm. -- (Designed for success)
Summary: Provides an overview of the design and engineering of racing motorcycles and road bikes.
Includes bibliographical references and index.
    ISBN 1-40340-773-8 (Library binding-hardcover)
    1. Motorcycles, Racing--Juvenile literature. [1. Motorcycles, Racing.
2. Motorcycle racing.] I. Title. II. Series.
    TL442 .G73 2003
    629.227'5--dc21
                            2002006122

Acknowledgments
The author and publishers are grateful to the following for permission to reproduce copyright material: pp. 1, 3, 11 (top), 13 (bottom), 14 (top), 23 (top) Alvey & Towers; p. 4 Dave Kimber/The Car Photo Library; p. 5 (top) John Noble; pp. 5 (bottom), 15 (top), 15 (bottom), 18 Auto Express; p. 6 EMAP; p. 7 (bottom) Suzuki PR Company; p. 8 MCN; p. 9 (top) MCN/EMAP; p. 9 (bottom) Gold and Goose; pp. 10, 14 (bottom) Unknown; p. 12 Triumph Motorcycles Ltd; pp. 13 (top), 24, 25 (bottom) R. D. Battersby; p. 16 Travel Ink; p. 17 (top) Yamaha; p. 17 Bob Battersby/Tograpix; pp. 19 (top and bottom) Eye Ubiquitous/Darren Maybury; p. 20 (left) Eye Ubiquitous/L. Fordyce; pp. 20 (right), 21 (bottom) The Ronald Grant Archive; p. 21 (top) Eye Ubiquitous/ Jonas Grau; p. 22 EPA; pp. 25 (top), 26, 27 (top), 28, 29 Corbis; p. 27 (bottom) Dave Campos; p. 29 Bettman/ Corbis.

Cover photograph reproduced with permission of Yamaha.

Every effort has been made to contact copyright holders of any material reproduced in this book. Any omissions will be rectified in subsequent printings if notice is given to the publishers.

Some words are shown in bold, **like this.** You can find out what they mean by looking in the glossary.

CONTENTS

FAST BIKES

There are many different types of motorcycles. Each type is designed for a different style of riding. Touring motorcycles are designed for comfort on long journeys, off-roaders are designed for fun on dirt tracks, and cruisers are designed for low-speed riding with ease.

However, in sports motorcycle design, **performance** comes first. Sports motorcycles are built to be thrilling to ride. They **accelerate** fast and hug the curves of the road and racetrack. Their size, weight, power, and shape are carefully designed to give them the exciting performance their riders desire. These high-performance motorcycles are often called superbikes. This is also the name of a type of motorcycle racing (see page 9) that is based on **production motorcycles.** Today, most of the world's motorcycles come from Japan and Italy. They are built by manufacturers such as Honda, Yamaha, Suzuki, and Kawasaki in Japan; and Ducati, MV Agusta, Laverda, and Cagiva in Italy.

FIREBLADE

When the Honda CBR900RR Fireblade was introduced in 1992, it started a revolution in sports motorcycle design. The Fireblade was lighter than older motorcycles, so it did not have to be as powerful. It was the first of a new generation of sports motorcycles whose light weight resulted in better sports performance. The Fireblade has been updated year after year.

Ten years after its introduction, the 2002 Fireblade is the lightest, fastest, and sportiest Fireblade yet. It has a 58.2-cubic-inch (954 cc) engine. This measurement shows how big the engine is.

NINJA

The Kawasaki ZX-12R Ninja's engine is bigger and more powerful than some car engines, but the bike is less than one-third of a small car's weight. The combination of its 73-cubic-inch (1,199-cc), 179-**horsepower** engine and light weight means the Ninja can reach a top speed of 180 mph (290 km/hr). This is almost as fast as a racing motorcycle. Like most sports motorcycles, it has a small windshield at the front to push air up and over the rider.

THE PURR-FECT CAT?

The Ducati 748 is sometimes described as "the perfect sports bike." Ducati is world famous for producing motorcycles with excellent performance and **handling.** Their motorcycles are as beautiful to look at as they are fun to ride. The 748 combines a great engine, graceful performance, and Italian styling. These features make it one of the world's most popular motorcycles among sports motorcycle fans.

Honda CBR954RR Fireblade

Engine size: 58.2 in.^{3} (954 cc)

Engine type: 4-cylinder **inline**

Engine power: 154 hp

Top speed: 185 mph (300 km/hr)

Weight: 370 lb (168 kg)

Wheelbase: 55.2 in. (1,400 mm)

SPORTS ROADSTERS

Sports roadsters are high-**performance** road motorcycles. They look similar to racing motorcycles and share many of the same design features.

The wheelbase (the distance between the front and rear wheels) is short. This makes the bike more **maneuverable.** The bike is made as lightweight as possible to give it faster **acceleration** and a higher top speed. The rear wheel is wider than the front wheel. This is important because the engine drives the rear wheel. A wider wheel means that as much of the wheel as possible contacts and grips the road. The more rubber that meets the road, the more engine power the wheel can transfer to the road.

SMOOTH RIDING

Sports motorcycle riders duck down behind the windshield, like a jockey perched on a racehorse. It is not easy. Riding with the weight on the hands can be quite tiring. They ride in this position because it offers the least **air resistance.** The motorcycle is also designed to cut air resistance. Its lumpy engine is surrounded by a **streamlined** cover, called a fairing, which deflects air smoothly around it. Cutting air resistance helps the bike go faster.

The Suzuki Hayabusa is named after a type of **falcon** that lives in Japan. In a dive, the bird can reach 200 mph (320 km/hr)—close to the top speed of the motorcycle.

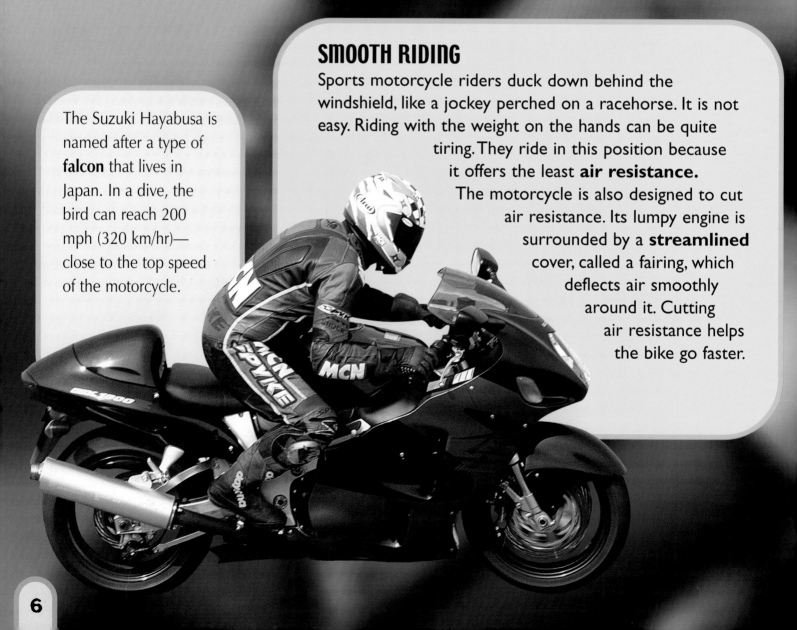

BRAKING DISTANCES

Sports motorcycles have disc brakes. They slow the bike down by gripping a disc fixed to each wheel. But the rider also has to read the road well. Higher speeds and wet and loose surfaces can more than double a motorcycle's **stopping distance.** Doubling a motorcycle's speed can increase the stopping distance by four times. A rider must also be careful not to brake too hard, because this could cause skidding.

dry road
—30 mph
(50 km/hr)

braking distance doubled

wet road
—30 mph
(50 km/hr)

speed doubled, braking distance increased four times

dry road
—60 mph
(100 km/hr)

SLICING THROUGH THE AIR

Designers of high-performance bikes such as the Suzuki Hayabusa have to consider how air flows around the rider as well as the bike and its engine. They use computer **simulations** of air flowing around a **virtual** motorcycle and rider to try different shapes and find out which works best. Then real models are tested in a **wind tunnel** before the bike is built.

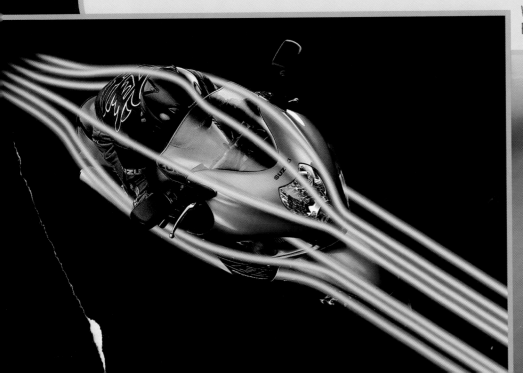

Suzuki GSX1300R Hayabusa

Engine size: 79.2 in.^{3} (1,298 cc)

Engine type: 4-cylinder **inline**

Engine power: 173 **hp**

Top speed: 200 mph (320 km/hr)

Weight: 474 lb (215 kg)

Wheelbase: 58.5 in. (1,485 mm)

RACING MACHINES

Many of the design features that make sports motorcycles so exciting to ride on the road were developed first for racing motorcycles. Racing motorcycles are divided into groups called classes. Each class has its own rules that cover things like engine size and the weight of the bike. They make sure that the bikes are closely matched in **performance** to make races more exciting. The challenge for designers is to create the best possible bike within the rules.

The **chassis** of a racing bike is especially important. It has to withstand the huge **acceleration,** braking, and cornering forces of racing without bending, twisting, or breaking. It also has to be as light as possible. It is very difficult to make parts that are both light and strong. However, it can be done by using lightweight materials such as **aluminum** or plastic. These materials are carefully shaped to give them extra strength.

GRAND PRIX

The leading two-wheeled racing class is called Grand Prix. It is for motorcycles with 30.5-cubic-inch (500-cc) engines. In 2001, Suzuki raced its RGV500-Gamma XR/B1 in this class. It was powered by a 30.5-cubic-inch, 185-**horsepower**, four-**cylinder** engine. It weighed only 290 pounds (130 kilograms). That's 65 to 90 pounds (30 to 40 kilograms) lighter than many 30.5-cubic-inch road motorcycles and more than twice as powerful. With so much power and such light weight, Grand Prix bikes can reach speeds higher than 185 mph (300 km/hr).

The motorcycle on the right is a Ducati 998F02 Superbike.

SUPERBIKES

One of the most popular racing classes is called Superbikes. Superbike racing motorcycles look similar to standard road motorcycles because strict rules limit how much the teams can modify them. As a result, success in Superbike racing often helps to sell more road motorcycles. The Italian motorcycle manufacturer Ducati has won more Superbike championships than all the other manufacturers put together.

Aprilia RS3 990 MotoGP racer

Engine size: 60.4 in.^{3} (990 cc)

Engine type: 3-cylinder **inline**

Engine power: 220 hp

Top speed: 200$^+$ mph (320$^+$ km/hr)

Weight: 300$^+$ lb (135$^+$ kg)

Wheelbase: 55.6 in. (1,410 mm)

NEW CLASS

A new racing class, called MotoGP, began in 2002. The Italian motorcycle manufacturer Aprilia created a new motorcycle for it. The rules say that a MotoGP motorcycle has to have an engine no bigger than 60.4 cubic inches (990cc), with at least three cylinders. The Aprilia RS3 990 is a 60.4-cubic-inch, three-cylinder model. Aprilia chose three cylinders because the rules allow them to make a three-cylinder bike lighter than one with four or more cylinders.

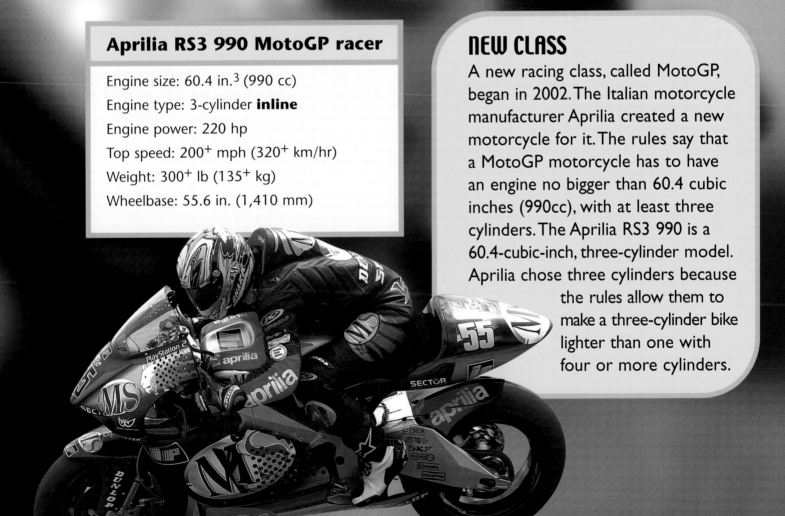

YAMAHA YZF-R1

DESIGNER DREAMS

A successful motorcycle begins with a design brief, which is a set of goals. The Yamaha YZF-R1's designers had three goals:
- to design the most powerful road-going sports motorcycle
- to make it lighter than its competitors
- to make it smaller than its competitors.

They started with a new four-**cylinder** engine. They laid it sideways across the motorcycle's width to make the motorcycle shorter. Then they added a new **chassis,** the motorcycle's main frame. A motorcycle's chassis has to be strong enough to keep it from twisting or bending. The Yamaha YZF-R1 is designed, like all modern motorcycles, so that the engine forms part of the chassis. The chassis reaches its full strength only when the engine is bolted to it.

LIGHTWEIGHT LIGHTNING SPEED

Slimming down parts and choosing the right materials saves weight. Saving weight is important, because a lighter motorcycle **accelerates** faster. Choosing a new type of plastic meant that the Yamaha YZF-R1's designers could make its **bodywork** lighter. They chose **titanium** instead of steel for the **muffler,** because titanium is lighter. By saving a few ounces here and there, pounds were shaved off the motorcycle's total weight. Once the design was completed, **prototypes** were built to test it.

muffler

fuel tank

chassis

engine

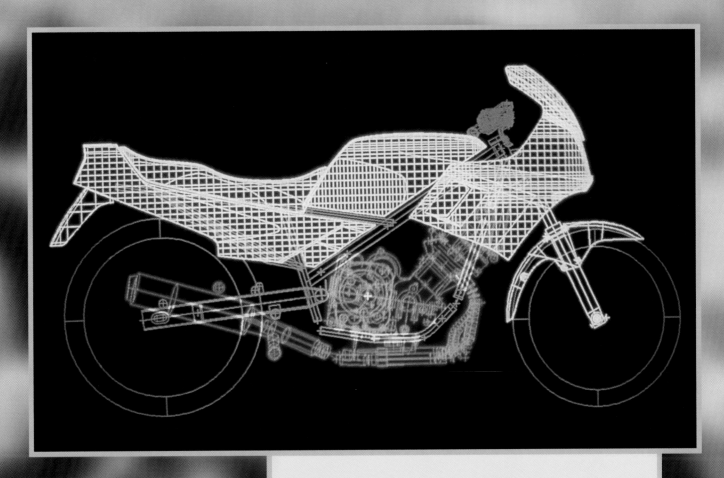

CAD

Computer aided design (CAD) speeds up the design of complicated machines such as the Yamaha YZF-R1. It can show problems at a very early stage. The designer can solve them before an expensive prototype is built.

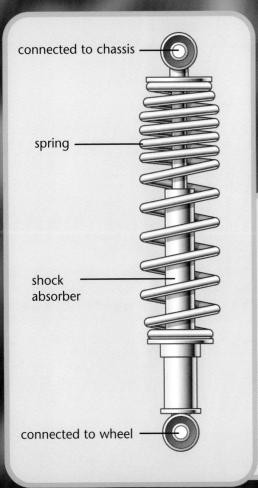

connected to chassis

spring

shock absorber

connected to wheel

SMOOTHING THE RIDE

It is important to keep a motorcycle's wheels on the ground because a wheel in the air cannot steer, brake, or transfer engine power to the road.

• Springs between the wheels and chassis give a smoother ride. They let the wheels follow bumps in the road without shaking the bike to bits.

• Each coiled spring works with a part called a shock absorber. The shock absorber's job is to stop the spring from bouncing too much, thereby keeping the wheel on the road.

YAMAHA YZF-R1

A GRAND PRODUCTION

Once the design team has done its job, the new design has to be turned into a motorcycle that people can buy.

Taking a motorcycle from a design on a computer screen to a **production** model has many steps. These steps have to be done in the right way at the right time. Standard **off-the-shelf** parts have to be ordered in the right numbers. Parts designed specially for the new motorcycle have to be made. A production line, where the motorcycle will be built, has to be set up. All the parts have to be delivered to the production line at the right time so that there are no delays. Meanwhile, the new model is shown to the public, so that everyone knows about it. Finally, thousands of the new motorcycles are sent out to dealers all over the world.

PRODUCTION LINE

Motorcycles are built on a factory production line, such as this one at a Triumph factory. Parts made in other factories are delivered to the production line and bolted together. In many factories, parts are moved around automatically to ensure that they are in the right place when needed. As each bike moves along the line, workers add more and more parts until a finished motorcycle is wheeled off the end. Every motorcycle is then checked and tested.

FROM SHIPPING TO SHOWROOM

Newly built motorcycles are packed in crates and loaded onto ships. The crates are specially designed to protect the bikes during their long journeys. The ships sail to ports all over the world. On arrival, they are unloaded and taken by truck to motorcycle dealers. There, they are uncrated and put on display in a showroom where customers can finally get a closer look at them.

GETTING THE MESSAGE OUT

Marketing is an important part of selling a motorcycle. The purpose of marketing is to tell people about the bike's design so that they will want to buy it. This involves telling people what the bike looks like, what its new design features are, and how well it performs.

- Ads placed in magazines are designed to give the motorcycle an attractive image.
- Brochures are sent to motorcycle dealers to give to their customers.
- The motorcycle itself appears at motorcycle shows, where people can see it.
- A few motorcycles are lent to writers at magazines so that they can write articles about them.

YAMAHA YZF-R1
DESIGNED TO PLEASE

Designers do not design only the parts of a motorcycle. They also design its **performance.** The Yamaha YZF-R1's performance has been carefully designed to please its riders.

The YZF-R1 has to give a thrilling ride, but it also has to be safe for the rider. Although it looks similar to a racing motorcycle, its designers have made it **handle** differently from a racing motorcycle. It **accelerates** quickly enough to be exciting, but not so quickly that it needs a professional rider to control it. Its **suspension** system is made soft enough to soak up bumps in the road, but hard enough to keep the bike from diving at the front when the rider brakes hard. A racing motorcycle's suspension is much harder, which can make it uncomfortable to ride and difficult to control, especially on rough ground.

RIDING POSITION

A sports motorcycle rider leans forward over the motorcycle's **fuel** tank. The shape of the YZF-R1 helps keep the rider in the right position. When the bike speeds up quickly, the rider is forced backward. The motorcycle's raised seat-back keeps the rider from sliding back. When a rider brakes hard, he or she is thrown forward. However, riders can hold firm by gripping cut-outs in the fuel tank with their knees.

raised seat-back

fuel tank cut-out

WHEELS

A motorcycle's wheels act like gyroscopes. A gyroscope is a spinning wheel that stays in the same position even if someone tries to turn it or push it over. The gyroscope effect helps to keep a motorcycle upright. However, the same effect also makes it harder to lean the bike over and make it turn. That is why you often see racing motorcyclists hanging off the side of their motorcycles, pulling them over to go around a corner. Yamaha made the YZF-R1's wheels lighter to reduce this gyroscope effect and make the bike easier to steer.

Designers have to be careful not to make a motorcycle either too easy or too hard to ride, or it won't have exactly the right sports performance its riders want.

Yamaha YZF-R1

Engine size: 60.9 in.^{3} (998 cc)
Engine type: 4-cylinder **inline**
Engine power: 152 **hp**
Top speed: 170 mph (270 km/hr)
Weight: 384 lb (174 kg)
Wheelbase: 55.0 in. (1,395 mm)

ENGINE POWER

One of the first decisions a motorcycle designer has to make is which type and size of engine to use.

Sports motorcycles need powerful engines for their graceful **performance.** The bigger and more powerful an engine is, the heavier it is, but sports motorcycles need to be light. Engine designers are constantly looking for ways of cutting the weight of an engine without reducing its power. Using lightweight **aluminum** instead of steel is one answer. Motorcycle engines work like car engines. **Fuel** and air are sucked into a **cylinder** inside the engine. A **spark plug** creates a spark that explodes the mixture. The hot gases spread out and push a **piston** down the cylinder. The up-and-down movement of the pistons in the cylinders drives the motorcycle's rear wheel. Most motorcycles have one to four cylinders.

TWIN POWER

The Harley-Davidson Springer Softail is powered by a popular motorcycle engine called a V-twin. It has two cylinders set at an angle, forming a V shape. The low rumbling sound of a big Harley V-twin is unmistakable.

THUNDERCAT

The Yamaha YZF600R Thundercat is powered by a four-cylinder **inline** engine. The cylinders are arranged in a straight line, just like a small car engine. Four cylinders deliver power to the wheels more smoothly than two cylinders.

COOL BOXER

The BMW R100 GS has a type of engine called a boxer. Most motorcycle engines have cylinders that stand up on end, next to each other. A boxer's cylinders lie flat, end-to-end across the width of the motorcycle. They are called horizontally opposed cylinders. A two-cylinder boxer is also called a flat twin. The wide shape of a boxer means that its cylinders stick out into the air rushing past the bike, keeping them cool.

cylinder

COOLING OFF

Burning fuel inside an engine heats up the whole engine. To keep it from heating up too much, it is cooled by using air or water.

- Most motorcycle engines are air-cooled. The cylinders are fitted with metal **fins** to give them a huge **surface area.** Air blowing around the fins absorbs some of their heat and carries it away.
- The biggest motorcycle engines are water-cooled. Water circulates through the engine and carries heat away to a **radiator.** Air blowing through the radiator cools the water, which goes back to the engine.

BMW R100 GS

Engine size: 59.8 in.³ (980 cc)

Engine type: Flat twin

Engine power: 60 **hp**

Top speed: 120 mph (190 km/hr)

Weight: 507 lb (230 kg)

Wheelbase: 59.7 in. (1,514 mm)

DRAG-BIKES

The fastest two-wheeled sport on a track is drag-bike racing. Drag motorcycles are designed to do one thing—**accelerate** as fast as they can in a straight line.

Drag-bikes do not have to turn corners or pass other motorcycles. They race two at a time down a straight track a quarter of a mile (402 meters) long. Like race cars, drag-bikes are divided into a series of classes. The fastest drag-bikes belong to the Top-Fuel class, which lets designers do almost anything in the search for speed. The challenge for the designer is to produce a machine that turns engine power into acceleration as fast as possible.

GETTING TIRED

A drag-bike's back tire is big and wide because it has to transfer a huge amount of engine power onto the track. Putting more rubber on the track gives better grip. Better grip means faster acceleration. The front tire is smaller and thinner. Its job is to keep the motorcycle going straight.

LYING DOWN ON THE JOB

A drag-bike rider lies down over the front of the bike. This not only cuts down **air resistance,** it also helps to weigh down the front of the bike. The engine is so powerful that it can lift the front wheel off the ground as the bike roars away from the starting line. Some bikes need the extra help of a long frame, called a wheelie bar, at the back to keep the front from rising up.

GSX1588 dragster

Engine size: 96.9 in.^{3} (1,588 cc)
Engine type: 4-cylinder **inline**
Engine power: 375 **hp**
Top speed: 185 mph (300 km/hr)
Acceleration: 0–60 mph (100 km/hr) in 1 second
Weight: 465 lb (211 kg)
Wheelbase: 78.1 in. (1,981 mm)

BURNING OUT

Soft rubber grips a track better than hard rubber, and rubber is softer when it warms up. So drag-riders warm up their big rear tires just before a race. They do this by a spectacular activity called burning out. With the front brake firmly applied so the bike does not move, the rider revs the engine so that the rear wheel spins against the ground. **Friction** between the tire and the ground heats the tire so much that clouds of thick smoke pour off it.

A drag-bike's rear tire does not last long. It may have to be replaced after only eight races. A Top-Fuel race can be over within five seconds, so a rear tire's lifetime may be less than one minute!

MODERN CLASSICS

New motorcycles appear nearly every month. They have the latest technology and materials, but not always the latest style or shape. Some riders prefer the classic styling of motorcycles from years ago. For these people, manufacturers make new motorcycles that look like those that were made up to 60 years ago. Making new motorcycles that look like old models is called **retro**-styling. Many of these motorcycles were made famous by Hollywood movies about young Americans growing up in the 1950s. The popularity of the films increased demand for the motorcycles ridden by their stars.

Harley-Davidson is one of the most successful manufacturers of retro-styled motorcycles. When British and then Japanese motorcycles flooded into the United States in the 1950s and 1960s, Harley-Davidson concentrated on making motorcycles with traditional styling. Their unique looks made them stand out from the rest. They were very successful, and they still are. Other manufacturers are now producing retro-styled motorcycles, too.

MOVIE MAGIC

Marlon Brando (right) looked cool and tough on his 39.7-cubic-inch (650 cc) Triumph Thunderbird in the 1954 movie *The Wild One*. Images like this, and of police officers on their Harley-Davidsons, created a demand for these motorcycles that has lasted to the present day.

KING OF THE ROAD

The Harley-Davidson Road King looks as if it came straight out of the 1950s. Although it looks like an old motorcycle, it is actually a modern motorcycle designed and built using today's methods and materials. Harley-Davidson produces more than a dozen motorcycles that have classic styling taken from the 1940s and 1950s.

CUSTOM DESIGN

Riders often try to make their motorcycles look a little different from everyone else's by adding different accessories. It is called personalizing or customizing. The height of the custom motorcycle craze was in the 1950s and 1960s, when the chopper motorcycle appeared. It was a motorcycle that was stripped down to only its most needed parts. Some choppers had long front **forks** and tall handlebars called ape-hangers. Many of these chopper motorcycles were based on Harley-Davidson models.

Harley-Davidson FLHR Road King

Engine size: 88.5 in.^{3} (1,450 cc)

Engine type: V-twin

Engine power: 67 **hp**

Top speed: 100 mph (165 km/hr)

Weight: 760 lb (345 kg)

Wheelbase: 63.5 in. (1,612 mm)

ACCIDENTS

No matter how well designed vehicles are, accidents still happen, because drivers and riders make mistakes. Riding a motorcycle is a fine balance of power and gravity. And things can go wrong.

A motorcycle on the road or the racetrack is usually under control only when both wheels grip the ground. A skid or a slide is bad news. Turning a corner too fast can make a motorcycle slide across the road. Turning on the power too quickly can make a wheel spin. Braking too hard can start a skid. Something mechanical can go wrong on the motorcycle. Even if the rider does not make a mistake and the motorcycle works perfectly, other people on the road can cause accidents. Moving vehicles have a lot of energy. The faster a vehicle goes, the more damage it can do if it comes to a sudden stop in an accident. That is why it is important to obey speed limits on public roads.

SLIDING OUT

A rider leans over in a turn to balance the cornering force that can topple the motorcycle. You can feel this sideways force when you turn a corner in a car. When a motorcycle leans over, it rides on the side of its tires. If the road is wet, oily, covered in gravel, or if the rider turns too fast, the tires lose their grip. The motorcycle slides toward the outside of the turn.

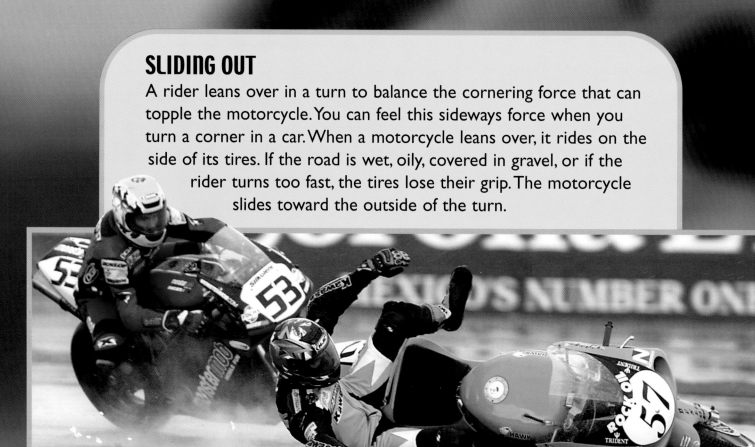

DIFFICULT TO SEE

Accidents involving motorcycles often happen because a motorcycle is so much smaller and narrower than many other vehicles. A driver who is passing other traffic or turning might not see a motorcycle, with disastrous results. Wearing bright clothing can help to make the motorcycle rider easier to see. Many motorcycles have lights that come on automatically when the engine is started.

KEEPING IT BALANCED

A motorcycle needs to be kept upright and balanced. The motorcycle's design helps the rider to do this. The heaviest part of a motorcycle is its engine. Keeping the engine as low as possible makes the motorcycle less likely to topple over. Imagine how much harder it would be to walk with a heavy backpack above your head instead of held down low.

SAFETY FIRST

Most drivers are protected inside their vehicles by seat belts, **air bags,** and soft surfaces. But a motorcycle rider has no protection. It is important that motorcyclists wear clothes designed to protect them if the worst should happen.

The most fragile part of anyone's body is the brain. So the most important piece of motorcycle safety gear is a helmet. It protects the head in three ways. The hard outer shell saves the head from injuries caused by crashing into a solid object. The soft lining inside the helmet cushions the head. Finally, a shatterproof visor shields the rider's eyes.

SKID LIDS

The most popular type of motorcycle helmet is the full-face type (left). It covers the whole head and face, and it has a clear visor on the front for the rider to look through. Some of these helmets have a flip-up front, so that the rider can talk to people without having to take the helmet off. Police motorcyclists sometimes wear this type. Riders of classic or **retro**-styled bikes often wear an older style of open-face helmet (right). It is called a jet helmet because it looks like a helmet worn by a fighter pilot.

WEARING LEATHER

A motorcycle racer wears a leather suit for two reasons. It protects the rider's body from scrapes and burns, and it also gives it a **streamlined** shape. This helps the air to slide smoothly over the rider's back. Reducing **air resistance** makes the motorcycle faster. This is important because races are often so close that saving a fraction of a second on each lap can make the difference between winning and losing.

WATCH YOUR BACK

After the head, the part of a rider's body that is most easily hurt is the spine. The **nerves** that control the arms and legs are inside the spine. That's why an injury to the spine can make a person unable to walk. Motorcycle racers and some road riders wear a hard pad, called a back protector or spine board, over their spine. Some leather motorcycle suits have a built-in back protector.

SUIT YOURSELF

The rest of the rider's body is protected by a tough jacket and pants. They protect the rider's skin from being scraped on the ground. Motorcycle racers and some road motorcycle riders wear a one-piece leather suit. Leather gloves and boots complete the outfit. Even with the best equipment, motorcycling can be dangerous, so riders have to be careful.

RECORD SETTERS

The motorcycles that set speed records look more like guided missiles than motorcycles. Their amazing shape helps them to go as fast as a small jet airplane! The faster a vehicle is designed to go, the more important its shape becomes. The right shape creates the least **air resistance** and lets the motorcycle go faster.

Long, slender motorcycles, called streamliners, set the fastest speed records. They pierce the air like an arrow. To squeeze as much engine power as possible into the slim body, they often have two engines, one in front of the other. Riders usually sit on top of a motorcycle, but land speed-record challengers are sealed inside their motorcycle so that they do not spoil the smooth flow of air over its body.

Land speed records are average speeds. The top speeds reached are much higher. The title of World's Fastest Motorcyclist is claimed by Jim Feuling. His Feuling Advanced Technologies motorcycle reached an official top speed of 332 mph (534 km/hr) on the Bonneville Salt Flats, in Utah, in 1997. Unofficially, the motorcycle is claimed to have reached a speed of 372 mph (595 km/hr).

BONNEVILLE SALT FLATS

Land speed records can be set only on a long, flat patch of ground. Motorcycle records have been set at the Bonneville Salt Flats since the 1950s. The area is baked by the summer sun, forming a hard, flat surface of 100 square miles (260 square kilometers). The black line in the photo is a guide for riders attempting to break records.

LIGHTNING BOLT

In 1978, Don Vesco set his fifth motorcycle land speed record. He reached 318 mph (512 km/hr) in his 123.6-cubic-inch (2,026cc) Kawasaki-powered Lightning Bolt motorcycle on the Bonneville Salt Flats. Later that year, he reached an unofficial top speed of 340 mph (544 km/hr).

EASYRIDERS

In 2002, the official motorcycle land speed record was held by Dave Campos. In 1990, he set a record of 322 mph (518 km/hr) on his Easyriders motorcycle on the Bonneville Salt Flats. Easyriders was 23 feet (7 meters) long and powered by two Ruxton Harley-Davidson engines. To set the record, Campos had to make two trips in opposite directions within one hour. Official timekeepers timed the two runs and figured out his average speed.

Easyriders land speed record holder

Engine size: 91 in.³ (1,491cc)
Engine type: 2 V-twins
Engine power: Unknown
Top speed: 322 mph (518 km/hr)
Weight: 2,500 lb (1,134 kg)
Wheelbase: 168.1 in. (4,267 mm)

DATA FILES

As we have seen, there are many different types of sports motorcycles. Each has been designed with a certain type of rider in mind. This table of information gives basic facts about some of today's best-known sports motorcycles.

Motorcycle	Engine size (in.³ / cc)	Engine power (hp)	Top speed (mph/ km/hr)	Number of cylinders	Weight (lb / kg)	Wheelbase (in. / mm)
Aprilia RS3 990 MotoGP racer	60.4 / 990	220	200+ / 320+	3	298+ / 135+	55.6 / 1,410
BMW K1200RS	71.4 / 1,171	130	124 / 200	4	628 / 285	61.3 / 1,555
Ducati 748	45.6 / 748	95	168 / 270	2	432 / 196	55.6 / 1,410
Easyriders record holder	91 / 1,491 (x2)	unknown	322 / 518	2 x 2	2.500 / 1,134	168.1 / 4,267
GSX1588 dragster	96.9 / 1,588	375	185 / 300	4	465 / 211	78.1 / 1,981
Harley-Davidson FLHR Road King	88.5 / 1,450	67	100 / 165	2	760 / 345	63.5 / 1,612
Honda CBR954RR Fireblade	58.2 / 954	154	185 / 300	4	370 / 168	55.2 / 1,400
Kawasaki ZX-12R	73.1 / 1,199	179	180 / 290	4	463 / 210	56.7 / 1,440
Suzuki GSX1300R Hayabusa	79.2 / 1,298	173	200 / 320	4	474 / 215	58.5 / 1,485
Triumph Daytona 955i	58.3 / 955	147	162 / 260	3	414 / 188	55.8 / 1,417
Yamaha YZF-R1	60.9 / 998	152	170 / 270	4	384 / 174	55.0 / 1,395
Yamaha YZF600R Thundercat	36.5 / 599	100	143 / 230	4	414 / 188	55.8 / 1,415

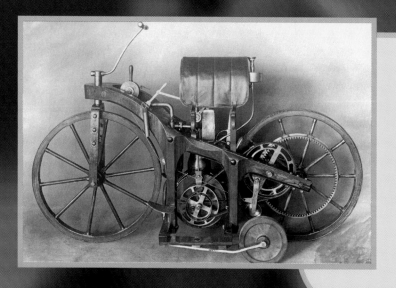

THE FIRST MOTORCYCLE

The very first motorcycle was not exactly a superbike. It was a heavy wooden vehicle with a 16.2-cubic-inch (265cc) engine built by the German engineer Gottlieb Daimler in 1885. It had a top speed of about 7.5 mph (12 km/hr). It needed two small stabilizer wheels to help keep it upright. There had been steam-powered bicycles as far back as 1869, but the Daimler motorcycle was the first to have a gas engine.

FURTHER READING

ABDO Publishing Company Staff. *The Ultimate Motorcycles.* Edina, Minn.: ABDO
Publishing Company, 1998.

Freeman, Gary. *Motorcross.* Chicago: Heinemann Library, 2002.

Hedrickson, Steve. *Supercross Racing.* Minnetonka, Minn.: Capstone Press Inc., 2000.

Passaro, John. *The Story of Harley Davidson.* North Mankato, Minn.: Smart Apple
Media, 1999.

Pupeza, Lori K. *Street Bikes.* Edina, Minn.: ABDO Publishing Company, 1998.

Raby, Philip. *Motorbikes.* Minneapolis, Minn.: Lerner Publishing Group, 1999.

Sievert, Terri. *The World's Fastest Superbikes.* Minnetonka, Minn.: Capstone Press, Inc.,
2002.

RACING

Motorcycle racing began in France in 1894. It quickly spread to other countries. The desire to win races encouraged motorcycle makers and racing teams to produce faster motorcycles. Many of the advances made for speed were later built into road motorcycles. The first races were held on regular roads. But soon race tracks were being built for both car and motorcycle races. The world's first race track was opened at Brooklands, in England, in 1907. The photograph on the right is of a motorcycle race at Brooklands in the mid-1920s.

GLOSSARY

accelerate to speed up. A motorcycle rider accelerates by twisting the handgrip at the end of the right handlebar. This feeds more fuel into the engine, which speeds up.

air bag safety device fitted to some cars. If the car crashes, an airbag in the steering wheel inflates in a fraction of a second and cushions the driver's head. Some cars have several different air bags in different places to protect passengers, too.

air resistance slowing effect of air on any object, including a motorcycle, that tries to move through air. Making a motorcycle smoother and streamlined reduces air resistance, allowing it to go faster.

aluminum lightweight metal that is easy to bend and shape. It is often used to make parts of motorcycles lighter than they would be if made from steel.

bodywork smooth outer shell of a motorcycle

chassis motorcycle's main frame. The rest of the motorcycle is bolted onto it.

cylinder tube-shaped part of an engine, where the fuel is burned

falcon bird of prey

fins thin pieces of metal attached to part of an engine to help cool it down. Air blowing around the fins absorbs some of their heat.

fork part of a motorcycle's suspension system. A spring and shock absorber inside a metal tube sit on each side of the front wheel, like two prongs of a fork.

friction force that tries to slow down moving objects when they slide over each other

fuel substance that is burned inside a motorcycle engine. This releases energy, which is converted into movement. Most motorcycles burn ordinary gasoline. Some drag-bikes burn special fuels designed to release energy even faster than normal gas.

handling how a motorcycle responds and holds the road when it is being driven

horsepower unit of measurement of the power of an engine, equal to the power to lift 550 pounds one foot in one second, or 746 watts of electrical power

inline type of engine with cylinders arranged next to each other in a row

maneuverable steerable. A more maneuverable motorcycle can make tighter turns than other motorcycles.

muffler part of a motorcycle's engine that reduces engine noise. The muffler is fitted to the engine's exhaust pipe or pipes. These carry waste gases out of the engine after the fuel has been burned.

nerves fibers that carry electrical impulses between the brain and other parts of the body. Information from the senses travels to the brain along nerves, and electric signals sent out by the brain to control the muscles also travel along nerves.

off-the-shelf ready-made. Off-the-shelf parts are existing parts that can be bought from a supplier and do not have to be specially designed and made.

performance how well a motorcycle works overall. A high-performance motorcycle is capable of faster acceleration and higher speeds than most motorcycles.

piston part of a motorcycle engine that slides up and down inside a cylinder. Burning fuel inside the cylinder pushes the piston down and drives the motorcycle's rear wheel.

production motorcycles motorcycles that are built in large numbers for sale

prototype first model of a new vehicle, built for testing

radiator part of an engine's cooling system. Water heated by the engine flows through thin pipes in the radiator. Air blowing around the pipes cools the water, which returns to the engine.

retro back or backward. A retro-style motorcycle is a modern motorcycle that looks like a motorcycle from the past.

simulation copy of an object, problem, or situation created inside a computer. A whole motorcycle can be created, or simulated, in a computer. It can then be tested to see how the real motorcycle will act in different conditions and at different speeds.

spark plug part of a motorcycle's engine that makes an electrical spark to burn the fuel in the cylinder. Each cylinder inside the engine has its own spark plug.

stopping distance distance a motorcycle travels between the time the rider applies the brakes until it comes to a stop

streamlined word used to describe a slim, smooth shape that moves through the air very easily

surface area size of the outside face of something. The fins on an air-cooled motorcycle engine are there to give it a bigger surface area, to give off more heat to the surrounding air.

suspension set of springs and other devices that connect a motorcycle's frame to its axles. The suspension system lets the wheels follow bumps and hollows in the ground, while the rest of the motorcycle moves along more smoothly.

titanium strong, lightweight metal that is used for making some parts of a motorcycle. Titanium does not rust, and it can withstand very high temperatures. It is also very expensive.

virtual not real. The plan, or design, of a motorcycle that appears on a computer screen is not real. It exists in the computer's memory and on the screen. It is a virtual motorcycle.

wind tunnel large tube or passage that air is blown through. Models of motorcycles and full-size motorcycles are tested by placing them in a wind tunnel and studying how air flows around them.

INDEX

DATE DUE

SEP 1 4			
NOV 1 2			
OCT 1 7			
OCT 2 4			
GAYLORD			PRINTED IN U.S.A.